OUT OF RANGE

Nick Drake's first collection, *The Man in the White Suit* (Bloodaxe Books, 1999), won the Waterstones Prize for Best First Collection, and was selected for the Next Generation Poets (2004). It was followed by *From the Word Go* (Bloodaxe Books, 2007), and *The Farewell Glacier* (Bloodaxe Books, 2012), a book-length poem which grew out of a journey to Svalbard in the Arctic to study climate change. The poem was recorded for *High Arctic*, an award-winning installation by United Visual Artists at the National Maritime Museum which ran through 2011. His latest collection is *Out of Range* (Bloodaxe Books, 2018).

Nick was also commissioned by United Visual Artists and Future Cities to create *Message from the Unseen World*, a poem for a permanent public art installation in Paddington Basin, commemorating Alan Turing. The text is available on his website.

He wrote the libretto for *Between Worlds* (ENO/Barbican, 2015), composer Tansy Davies, director Deborah Warner; and for *Cave* (London Sinfonietta/Royal Opera House, 2018), composer Tansy Davies, director Lucy Bailey, performed at the Printworks, Canada Water. The text is available on his website.

His plays include *All the Angels* (Faber) at the Wanamaker Theatre at Shakespeare's Globe; *To Reach the Clouds*, Nottingham Playhouse; and *Success*, National Theatre Connections Project, at the Olivier, and around the country.

He wrote the screenplay for the film *Romulus My Father*, starring Eric Bana, directed by Richard Roxburgh, which won four awards at the Australian Film Institute Awards, including best film.

www.nickfdrake.com

NICK DRAKE

Out of Range

BLOODAXE BOOKS

ISBN: 978 1 78037 428 4

First published 2018 by
Bloodaxe Books Ltd,
Eastburn,
South Park,
Hexham,
Northumberland NE46 1BS.

www.bloodaxebooks.com
For further information about Bloodaxe titles
please visit our website and join our mailing list
or write to the above address for a catalogue

Supported using public funding by
**ARTS COUNCIL
ENGLAND**

Cover design: Neil Astley & Pamela Robertson-Pearce.

Printed in Great Britain by Bell & Bain Limited, Glasgow, Scotland, on
acid-free paper sourced from mills with FSC chain of custody certification.

We have no words for the darkness. It is not night, it is not ignorance. From time to time we all cross this darkness, seeing everything, so much everything that we can distinguish nothing...

JOHN BERGER

Blue is the colour of longing for the distances you never arrive in, for the blue world.

REBECCA SOLNIT

Nature loves courage

TERENCE McKENNA

ACKNOWLEDGEMENTS

'From the Song Dynasty' and 'Ollamaloni' were commissioned by *The Guardian* in response to the Royal wedding (2011) and the London Olympics (2012) respectively. 'Chronicle of the Incandescent Lightbulb' first appeared in *Energetic: Stories of Change* (OU/Shed)

Heartfelt thanks to John Mole and Jackie Kay, whose close reading helped me at every stage. To Helen and John Kay – thanks for the wonderful journeys and the songs. Thanks to Nancy Campbell, Bob Davies, Dave Stagg and Simon Coury for their invaluable responses. To Bevis Sale for inspiration and ideas, and John Frankland for introducing me to Terence McKenna. Loving thanks to my partner Edward Gonzalez Gomez for sharing the years of these poems.

CONTENTS

Through the Red Light

I saw him at rush hour, courier
appearing from the primordial chaos
of the underpass into the dawn array's
thousand windscreens mirroring the sun,

on the spooky geometry of his racing bike,
cans clamped to his head, ticks on his heels,
stubble glitter-gold on his cool face,
not giving a flying fuck about red lights –

As he scanned me sideways with a passing
glance I swear I caught a shock of light,
a handful of sparks, wild fire in the pixelated
secret of his eyes – then the red turned green

but he was out of range, zigzag
zooming away as everyone gave chase

Inklings

A clue of next to nothing. An engine turning
over and over on a winter morning.

A hair's breadth in the mouth. The way a lover
eats that scrawls an X across your love.

The punch line and the standing non-ovation.
A contrail that never quite fades back to blue.

The final straw of plastic on a broken ocean.
A knock on the door that breaks the heart

of the silence. A coin of almost no
denomination balanced on your tongue.

A day that dawns when everyone wears black,
the sky red, in the distance your home town

across a dark river. The congregated inklings
whisper their spell: *lightning, thunder, rain…*

Chronicle of the Incandescent Lightbulb

You had nothing but the moon,
the guttering candle, and the dish of oil
to thread the eye of a needle, read,
or cast shadows on the walls, until
you created us, the first light
that was constant in the darkness.

From a heart-beat twist of tungsten
and a single breath of gas to hold
our whole lives long, you sowed
one idea in our glass skulls;
to shine at your command.

We shed no tears of wax; reliable,
disposable, we lived where you lived,
lit your parties and wars; one by one
we brightened the hill shanties
and towers of your mega-cities;
when you were lost, we were home
waiting, just a click away
to save you from the small hours' fears;
when your lives hung by a thread
we stayed as long as necessary;
we shone when you were gone.

When the invocation of our filament
broke with a secret *tick*
you cast us off – and now you wish
a light perpetual and free,
your highways and cities radiant
archipelagoes against the dark.

But if the lights go out from time to time,
lie back on the black grass, gaze up
at the banished constellations, take
ancient starlight in, and listen
for the dark song of our source summoning,
on summer nights and winter afternoons,
the antiquated powers of the moon.

Maenad

Outside the station, a raving statue
confronting the commuter stream's current,

her mouth erupting with syllables
of grief and fear as we hurried by,

ignoring or dreading her desperate appeals
for someone to *please just fucking listen!*

Something about a child, an emergency
to get to a hospital, *why won't anyone help?*

AM I INVISIBLE OR SOMETHING?
When someone stopped she sobbed with gratitude.

And then I saw her a few days later, the same
tragic performance, mask of agony,

hair scraped back, black leggings, boots
unlaced, eyes crazed, at her wits' end

again. I looked at her, and she screamed
don't you fucking smile at me you CUNT!

Her accusations raged at my back
until at a safe distance I turned,

to see her kicking the indifferent wall,
pleading on the phone, her cigarette's

hot tip scribbling on the winter air,
not an actress backstage on her scene break,

but a girl crying the street, incendiary,
her fury bright as phosphorus in rain.

Still Life: Plastic Water Bottle (used)

Why did you
make us in
your image?

Replicants
of the prototype, not
goddesses of ancient fertility,
not glass, clay, wood or stone, but
generated from dark matter in a split
second to join the silent masses,
monks, soldiers, clones, waiting
in the moonlight of the fridge
for you to drink down our short
stories of healing waters and bright
sugars until our emptiness
is complete – but there
we part: cast off, we colonise
every dominion from the highest peak
to the deepest fathom of the abyss
and though the timeline of the waves
degrades us to nanoparticles, yet
we will survive all the brief histories
of your unsuccessful flesh to abide
in every living heart undying...
Now only you can save us from
the doldrums of this everlastingness
if you conceive a new skin of beautiful
mortality that grants us too the strange
sea-change of release
into the mercy of everything
and nothing

Ollamaloni

(Aztec: Rubber Ball Game)

To celebrate the London Olympic Games

I send you this report
and risk your disbelief;
in the stone stadium
of their temple of sacrifice
teams of very nearly naked men
gleaming with oil,
back to back, waited
until the crowd was silenced
as at the Gloria of our Church
when the Holy Spirit is invoked.
What happened next defies
all reason; I saw it spring from Nothing
then leap across the sky into the sun;
at first I thought it was a wingless bird
spinning and vaulting in joy
like our swallows; but it fell to earth,
kissed the stone, and then flew up again –
the men gave chase, but the creature
tricked them, gathering speed
with every bound, rising ever higher –
the congregation roared, and I confess
tears poured down my face –
I know not why; only my ardent faith
prevented me from stripping off
my black soutane, and joining in the fray.
In the spirit of enquiry I desired
to hold the object of the game.

They gave it to me. I have it now
in the palm of my hand,
a small, dark globe, warm
as an egg, or a new-fallen star,
and decorated with skulls;
heavy as a stone, and yet
what spirit moves it? Whose god
created such a wonder
that leaps for joy? And why
does my body tremble with delight
to play the game again?
Pray for me now –
for I find I cannot let it go.

Dance

Scene: two men at the crowded bar of a gay club.
Behind them, countless shirtless figures dance under strobe lights.
Time: around 3 a.m...

I prefer natural bodies, he says; not these
gym-formed raving muscle queens, eyes closed
and off their heads on the dance-floor of mirrors,
oh please – and as for those other genres
that speak of the call of the wild, the bears
discussing their beards, urban cowboys
boogying in strict lines under glitter-balls,
skinheads from gentrified postal codes
going Yeah? What's it to you? And then
the slings and arrows in suburban dungeons,
candle-wax slowly dripped exactly so,
the avant-garde negotiating how near
a human fist can touch the soul – oh boys!
What are we searching for, what ecstasy
do we crave from the poor mortal body
and its holy shrines where we kneel and pray
to the hidden god, the porntastic ideal
incarnate of our fantasies; is it the true
touch of the divine, or its sorrow realised
in the lineaments of our ever-failing flesh?

Kick back, baby, he replies. It's just sex;
it's play, it's fun, it's pleasure, all night long;
just let it go and join the human race;
loosen up. Shut up. Take this. Kiss me. Dance –

The Palace of Memory

Demolished, now a coffee shop, offices.
Rebuild it word by word, from the street

up the sticky stairs, buzzed through the door
into the shanty plywood labyrinth of cabins.

Clink of watches, wallets, wedding rings
deposited in the insecure lockers.

Undressing, shedding work-skins, zips, socks.
Transformations into nakedness.

The democracy of laundry-aged towels,
the magic trick, withholding and revealing,

tightened, loosened, draped, to part, to fall.
Bodies of all the ages, muscles, flab,

ceaseless pacing of the corridors,
entrances and exits of the steam room,

water running in the shadow showers,
aromas of ammonia, poppers, sweat.

And then the grazing hand, the shaken head
or nod. Locked doors, vinyl mattresses,

mutters, whispers, confidences, sometimes
a laugh in the dark, a sob, a *Jesus, fuck…*

We might have loved each other; in our heads
we dreamed this place up as we came and went,

nameless strangers, sudden intimates, nude
ghosts walking through the office walls.

From the Song Dynasty

(17th April 2010)

The tale survives of two men
who fell in love 'at first sight';
who shared everything
in unbounded intimacy
including the pillow
and the red embroidered coverlet
which had been in the family
for generations.
Whether they had bad days,
domestic arguments
or inappropriate dreams
we do not know –
no doubt such burrs
were worked away by time
polishing its story;
how they found each other
and lived together all their lives,
and died on the same day,
and were buried by the grieving town
on Mount Luofo's peak
with their pillow and red coverlet;
and how a pine tree grew
out of the grave
like the character for longevity
and true love.

Such is the legend.
I like to think of them,

Pan Zhang and Wang Zhangxian,
in the crowd of well-wishers
waiting in the April sunshine,
perhaps under white cherry trees
in full bloom, like us
here and now, on this day
early in the twenty-first century
with our new rings
of silver and rose gold
growing warm on our fingers.

With Helen and John at Kelvingrove

The plate glass windows of the new café frame
children kicking through the autumn's hoard
of big plane tree leaves made from one bold stencil
in red, green and gold. In her beret

and matching purple scarf Helen wonders
at their wild delight. At our table, the happy
plethora of soup bowls, tea pots and cake plates
of her birthday celebration. After lunch

John guides me to the upper galleries
and the Dutch Lesser Masters – 'Ay, they're the ones' –
as he talks me down a row of tiny
gilt-framed windows into umber chambers,

pubs and backrooms where, the wall-label says,
'Drunks and prostitutes pose as a music party.
Encouraged by tobacco and alcohol
the music was probably not very good.'

John reads this out, delighted and appalled –
'Unless, mebbe, the Dutch Lesser Masters
could only afford as willing models
the working classes!' Composed in this odd genre

depicted in the pigments of the poor
for the leisured patrons' patronising gaze
their faces seem weird with mirth – either
the wine-bribed victims of the painter's hoax

or sharing a piss-take complicity,
so not the inferiors of the bourgeoisie
but its comedians – 'Ay, the joke's on who?'
John chuckles, the brightest man I know,

with the memory of a public library.
Arm in arm we stroll the galleries
with Helen and Jackie until we stand together
before Francis Cadell's *A Lady in Black*;

enigmatic, between coming and going,
she waits in a cool grey hall in gold gloves,
pink roses and a Chinese blue vase on the table,
her back to a large gilt mirror, her face turned

to gaze away, oblivious of us all,
attired in a black velvet coat and hat
in which the side-ways winter light construes
cobalt, madder, viridian and silver grey.

The day fades as we say goodbye; John Kay,
blue shirt, red sweater, tweed jacket, ninety-three,
bestows, not cheek to cheek, but man to man,
a twinkling, farewell kiss, fond on my lips.

Saturday Morning

(at the Cable Café)

We are figures disposed in sunlight
each with one white cup
of excellent coffee.

The sugar shakers shine,
and all is laptop silence, until
a man in nothing but cut-off jeans

enters like a king to beg a light;
the young woman behind the counter asks
Did you lose your shirt?

And he shouts *Normally I'm a nudist!*
We all laugh suddenly,
and he retires, revelling

to the promenade of the street
bowing to the angels at the bus stop,
saluting the glorious sun.

London Fields

This country's gone to the fucking dogs!

He bellows at us on Sunday in the park,
in our enchantments of affluence and style –

And I think – old mad white man ranting, rage, blow –

And now they fucking lock the fucking toilets
on Sundays – what the fuck is that about?

His soliloquy unravels, but he's right,
the toilets are shut, so where else
is he supposed to do a shit's necessity...

While his dog, poor cringing boy, stays by the bench
faithfully guarding the unaccommodated spot

he hurries across the grass, behind a tree
for the bare dignity of it, and squats –

For Sandra

(b. ? 1998, d. Jan 2016)

You never curled into my neck, or wound yourself
round and round in my lap like an idea
seeking its ideal expression in a circle
of sleep. You were not that kind of cat.

Little survivor, dubious, nervous,
lover of sun on warm stone, pretend huntress
of imaginary flies; but mostly terrified
of the peril beyond the cat-flap's mystery.

Too old and ill to live, I set you down
on the cold steel table, in the filthy blanket
you'd slept on for years, and spoke my poor
last words in silence because I felt ashamed

in front of strangers to say; *you've been a great cat
and we love you.* Then I nodded, the vet
inserted the needle, you sipped on three last breaths
and, as on a gentle comma, you were gone...

And it seemed your little spirit instantly darted
through the needle-eye of our hearts, for we wept
like children as we stroked you on and on
as if to help you, little cat, to *go* –

join the great stream of life dying today,
all the single creatures congregating
in the ark of this winter moon; then fly away
beyond the constellations to meet the dark.

Peaches for the Solstice

(for Edward Gonzalez Gomez)

Six peaches from the all-night store; I saw them
angled to the array of fluorescent lights,
sunset red in their soft blue cardboard beds
that safeguarded their journey from the trees
in some imaginary ancient orchard, probably
via the cargo belly of a 747,
to their brief still-shelf-life of doubtful ripeness
in the Star and Palm emporiums of London.

Lucky to live in a city where you can buy
peaches at midnight on the summer solstice –
each one might be a sweet or damaged sun,
and only part of this world cornucopia
of apricots, cherries, pineapples, pomegranates,
watermelon crescents, bunches of dusty grapes,
composed between the pavement and the window
like provisions for a prosperous after-life.

Lucky to live in a city where young men
go hand in hand into the trendy bars,
and buses pass by like lit theatre scenes;
in dark parks lovers star-gaze, smoke and laugh,
and reggae counteracts the sirens' cries
of inequality and emergencies;
the city's imbalances and tipping points just
held, on this night of light's high-tide.

The imperfect is our paradise; tonight
I'll make a wish to the democratic moon
in her shimmery glamour of tarnished air
hung above the traffic and tower blocks
in summer's marquee of light-bulbs and planes –
long life, good luck, love and happiness;
on the shortest night, under the festival stars
let's share these peaches I bought home for us.

The Flies

You praise the bees for their industry and honey
as if they were poets of the sun, and we
barbarians who couldn't give a shit
about flowers; you revile us as evildoers

of the hot, fly-blown seasides of decay;
blue bottles, green bottles, punk
scavengers, embezzlers, outsiders
inside, obsessed with the small print, always

missing the high window of freedom
behind us, above us, over and over, trapped
on a vertical stage of glass –
forever on the wrong side of the light.

But your war zones and panoramas of disaster
are famously our fields of treasure,
your sufferings and little cries, our data;
we scent death's augury from ten miles away;

arriving at the scene before ravens, before crows,
before all other reporters, we get
the breaking story; we worship and adore
the half-life of flesh, fear's salts, tears' spirits,

and observe from every hidden camera angle,
zoom-lensed, fast-forward shutter speed, to catch
your command performances of love and death –
for every ointment, a fly; why?

Because no matter how many you kill
in unholy battle, or the numberless who lie
on the memorial of the windowsill,
we are with you, as it always was

and ever shall be; we are more like you
than you care to know; time is wound tight
as revenge in our concentrated hearts;
summer's light is brief, and there is much to do

in the great work of our master;
not in the harmonious hum of the chantry hive,
but in the ceaseless buzzing of the air,
and the long silence of your open mouths.

Shame

When I tried to confess the wonders
I discovered in my heart,
they dressed me in shadows,
covered my eyes, denied my face,
tied my beautiful hands into fists
and chained my dancing feet
to the stone of their hate.
I became a small, dark tree,
leafless, in winter;
and while they cursed, I sang.
And although they tried
they could not catch that bird,
so they set fire to me,
to the tinder of my secrets,
and the love letter of my skin,
and the conflagration of my hair;
I remember the roar of the black air,
the wind's fury in the chimney
of my bones, and the bird
taking flight, disappearing
into silence.
Now they have nothing
but the handful of ash
that remains of me
to cast into the air.

In Medellín

From my hotel window
I watch the boy in the street
dressed in rags like the polluted feathers
of a flightless bird brought low
on the hot pavement,
crouched, hunched
his face sunk
into his knees
against the mid-day sun
and the crowds in the plaza;
ten feet away
a plot of watered grass
and palm trees offer crowns of shade for free –
benches face the fountain's
altar of water;
but for his own reasons he prefers
to balance
on the long tight-rope of shadow cast
by a lamp post
across the grey-pink stones
like a wire-walker
staring down
at the gods of the abyss.

Night Bus

When I get up for a glass of water,
throat dry, mind stuck in the small hours'
lunacies, someone is shouting – a shadow

outside the bus stop's lit canopy,
standing in the dark rain calling out
lamentations to the empty street –

What words in what language is he yelling
across time zones and distances?
How far is home? He sounds like a man

forgotten by everyone, and God.
He hops from foot to foot, it's not a dance,
but sad steps that require too much strength.

Is he howling for his dead in their distant graves?
Or a man solitary in an indefinite prison
protesting against injustice and corruption?

Or calling out hope's broken promises
for those killed walking home, for those
whose ground constantly shifts and gives way?

Why don't I put my coat on, get my keys,
cross the road, ask are you OK, what
can I do, come in, sit at my kitchen table?

Would he stare at me, eyes crazed with ghosts, and speak?
But I'm too afraid to let his keening in
unless it were a moon-sick blues, and the rain

a kora or an oud accompanying him,
transposing his grief to music, his howl to song...
So when a silent ambulance's blue light flashes past

I retreat to the kitchen for my glass of water.
And when I look again he's disappeared.
Perhaps the night bus came. Perhaps he's

riding it now, at the front of the upper deck,
the magician of his own life's journey,
the night city all before him; perhaps he's safe

with the others sleeping, going home, or not,
faces covered against the heartless lights,
leaning against the glass, against the rain.

Driving to Achiltibue

(for Helen, John and Jackie)

As if we are remembering this together;
John is trying to reconcile the mountains
in our windscreen's panorama

to the names on the map. There is a problem of scale.
Helen lays back her lovely head
and gazes at the dreamland as the road

winds us further and deeper and quieter away,
past the *lochans* with their tiny unnamed islands,
lenses ruffled by interstellar breezes,

and the crenellated cliffs and hanging keeps
tipped west and heaved, stone against light,
which once were grains of sand under an ocean

long gone. There is a problem of scale. Helen and John
sing Woody Guthrie, and MacCaig's line
Who owns this land? is in John's mouth; *Aye*

good question! he chuckles… Jackie and me
catch each other's eye in the rearview mirror;
and then we're driving back through time's silence

to the oldest place in the west, the moor
an old girl dwelling under her worn, tan cloak,
squinting at the sky, examining her dreams,

the sea in her mouth, the shingle of the names –
Stac Pollaidh, Sula Bheinn, Cul Mor, Cul Beag –
as she puts the kettle on the sun to boil;

and this road, this day, this hour, Helen and John,
Jackie and me, go hand in hand with her song –
I bhi à bhi ù bhi à bhi, i bhi a bhi ù bhi à bhi

sorrowing and skipping, singing us back home.

Cormorants

(for Jackie)

Mid-morning, walking along the strand
to buy the Sunday papers from the village shop,

we'd paused to admire the bus stop timetable
(one daily arrival and departure) and the cormorants

diving, disappearing, remerging,
vigilant. But then we noticed the dim

phantom of the conning tower cruising
incognito through the glitter of the loch

carrying its codes and crews to sea.
Neither of us knew what to say.

We remembered John and Helen, brave
protesters at the gates of the print-out base,

ring-fenced, barb-wired; arrested, roughed up, held
a night in the cells. Fined ten pounds each

thirty-five years ago. As we walked back
with the papers under our arms, faint ripples

arrived lapping the shoreline like the sonar
wake of an underwritten story.

The cormorants continued with their endeavour,
stitching a sampler from the peaceful water.

Out of Range

Up here there is no signal;
it died at the cattle grid
where even the trees can't pass.

In the listening station of these hills
bracken has its own system
to intercept the clandestine

wavelengths of streams and airs;
and the rain's dark radiance
registers its impressions

on stonewalls and grey rocks
where highly sensitive mosses
gather the information of the stars.

At night, in the pitch black
of the wrong side of the moon
I stand with my fading torch

in the last phone box on earth,
a windowed coffin, a haunted mini-crypt
where a spider's devised seven webs

then died inside the phone;
for down this cold receiver
which smells of strangers, mouth to mouth,

your voice is five thousand miles away;
so I shout *can you hear me? I love you, I love you*
until I hear through the rush-hour babble

of horns, airbrakes and squawking parrots
your delayed echo *I love you too*
while here I stand

in this crazy dark, feeding my last coins
to the insatiable seconds
counting down to silence.

Anubis

(i.m. Paul Sussman, archaeologist, novelist, 1966-2012)

God/dog!
Here are offerings; champagne, cakes, meat;
the best of everything we have in this world – take it
and let us pass; but say which way he went
into the House of Dust – or better still
let our lament persuade you; guide us down
between the shadows of the Otherworld,
lead us through the dead woods, and defend us
from the Fears carved into dripping rock and dark;
whisper in our ears the chants and prayers,
the backward spells, the spells of secret names,
to calm them back to sleep in their cold beds.
And when we stand in the Hall of Judgment, please
petition the silent goddess as she waits
before the balanced scale of souls, and say;
here are the pieces of our broken hearts;
we only want him back, this once, for now,
for a day, even for five minutes, for one second
so we can breathe him in before he's gone...

And as the white feather of truth drifts down
in the silence, in the balance...

CUT TO:

The festival of his memorial; outside
the light of a summer evening is running;
three auditorium walls go dark, the fourth
illuminates; white light flickering becomes

Paul's face recurring, his smile revived, his heart
beating at 35 frames per second,
smiling and waving from the Otherworld
at life, now that he has no part in it –
but sends us all his love, his love, his love…

The image skitters, sticks; the wall's a wall,
a time-locked dead-end stop; no words or spells
can conjure back the light in which he lived.
So go now, dog/god, back into the shadows;
go hungry; disappear into the dark.

The Foley Artist (take 2)

'A specialist in creating sounds, especially of body movement, recorded to fit the pictures on the screen.'

A strange calling; to play the minor effects,
the off-screen score you'd notice by its absence;
but in this small suitcase of tricks I hold
the bric-à-brac of people being there –
the world dismantled to its sticks and stones.
For instance, I can conjure my own approach
from foggy distances with a handful of pebbles;
paper torn is fire; an ounce of sand
hissing in a matchbox is the sea,
or the Sahara, or a deep sleep.
Ten raindrops caught in zero gravity
concoct a storm. A grain of salt is tears.
Mystery is velvet, silver-nitrate night.
With ebony, feathers, needles, smoke and dust
I have mastered all the little noises of war.
It is my music. Time is two tin hands,
or a splinter of moon-rock and its tidal pull,
or breath mist fading on an inch of mirror.
I could articulate the life and death
agonies of a snowflake, or this – my invisible grin.
Imagine me now, alone in my dark room,
no words, no music, and no audience –
a hyperactive, loony one-man-band
tinkling, jingling, rattling, scratching, banging
to the tempos of shadow and light,
from small Genesis to third act Apocalypse...
And when I reach the last, stuttering frames;
a balloon twisted awry's a question mark;

a football rattle, cranked, is dying breath;
and the great arcana of smoke-rings are
the loop-holes through which I disappear
as if I was never here...

                        But this is just 'The End' –
for after the diminishing credits, and the theme-tune
reiterated by the immortal orchestra,
hot white light unravels, which requires
for the scratchy quarks and strangeness of lost time
a bike wheel's bust spokes tickering slowly down.
And for those remaining in the audience
loyal to the end beyond 'The End'
who have nowhere else to go, except out
into the snow that's falling in the world
beyond the screen, beyond this velour box,
falling in the winter of forever...
it's here the limit of our art is truly tested
for the secret of the final mystery is
the sound we only make after we've gone.

The Dancing Satyr

(Royal Academy, Bronze exhibition.)

Wild hair, pointed ears, tail missing, bronze skin changed
to the turquoise and viridian of the cold, bright sea
where you lay wrecked for twenty-five centuries,

alabaster eyes gazing up at the boiling dream-mirror,
then caught in the night nets of local fishermen, so the story's told,
and raised like a damaged question mark to now.

One leg shattered, both arms gone, twisting torso still
leaping like the dancer of a pandemonium
through hushed museum air and whispering mortal crowds –

strange creature, extraterrestrial, seven-foot tall wonder,
singing in ecstasy or uttering a modem feedback
at a pitch too extreme for human ears to hear –

a warning of the future's dark tsunami
into which we're running backwards, oblivious
as it sweeps away our cities and our dreams?

Raving incensed, deranged, flayed skin, tiny cock,
smashed skull, a hole for nil by mouth, disaster survivor
of the nano-second of the shattering explosion

resuscitated but refusing to answer our interrogations,
say what you've seen, or your name, or what happened,
or the last thing you remember, or for God's sake *why?*

Or insomniac wild thing, off your head, thrilled
by the never-never heart-beat of each epileptic flash
of the strobe and moonflower disco inferno,

party animal, nature boy, with all your love to give,
slipping through the crowd of reaching hands
to disappear through the red curtains of dawn rain?

No answer. Keep your secrets. No human kiss
can give you breath, turn metal into skin – but you don't care;
long after we've gone you rave the empty gallery

and we're *your* dream as you dance the deepest blue
to the sea's shanty, wind in the woods, to Earth's lost songs
in the radiant silence of the boundless dark.

Self-portrait as a Moose

A difficult incarnation – sensitive
outcast with the long face carrying
a dull bell of dejection round his neck.

He wears a shaman's velvet crown of horns.
From between the prison bars of winter trees
he stares a thousand yards in empty prayer.

He strips a branch with one slow lyric lick.
To dine on dandelions, one by one, he
bows and steps back across the meadow.

His upper lip is velvet, meticulously
prizing emerald moss and rusty lichens
discerned beneath the hush and drift of snow.

He licks the tribute of salt from icy roads.
In summer ponds he stands like a sun king
disregarding his reflection in the mirror.

Sometimes he comes to a halt for no
obvious reason. Children are told
he dances in moonlight, but this is never seen.

Three Arctic poems

1

Fold up the charts.
Close the guidebooks
and the scrolls
of information.
Turn the engines off.
Let the laptop
sleep.
Let your wristwatch
stop.
Let plans and speculations
and the names of things
go –

Pick up a stone
and hold it in your hand;
this is the history
of the world –

Watch the animal of the light
always moving away
across the land
in its own time –

And when the darkness comes
welcome it
for it makes you think
and dream.

II

I am a long story,
ten thousand feet long,
a hundred thousand years old,
a chronicle of lost time
back to the first dark,
too dark for telling;
I am every winter's fall;
I am the keeper of the air
of all the vanished summers;
I honour the shadows of sorrows
that come to lie
between my pages;
I distil lost atmospheres
pressed into ghosts
kept close to my cold
old heart.

And as for you –
what story would you like to hear?
On your two feet,
tracking the snow
two by two, two by two, two by two;
here is the dust and music
of your brief cities;
here is the ash and smoke;
here are your traffic jams
and vapour trails;
here are your holidays in the sun
and your masterpieces
and your pop songs;
here are your first cries

and last whispers;
here are your long sighs
of disappointment;
here is where it went right,
and where it went wrong.
Easy come. Easy go.

So I know why you slice
moon after moon from me,
holding each fragile face
up to your searchlights;
why you measure and record
the tiny cracks and snaps
of my mysteries:
because you fear
you are the people
who have changed nature –
and now you are on your own.

I have no more to tell.
No questions please
about the future
for now the great narrator
Silence
takes over;
listen carefully to her story
For you are in it.

III

Dear mortals;
I know you are busy with your colourful lives;
you grow quickly bored,
and detest moralising;
I have no wish to waste the little time that remains
on arguments and heated debates;
I wish I could entertain you
with some magnificent propositions and glorious jokes;
but the best I can do is this:
I haven't happened yet; but I will.
I am the future, but before I appear
please, close your eyes, sit still
and listen carefully.
I can't pretend it's going to be
business as usual.
Things are going to change.
I'm going to be unrecognisable.
Please, don't open your eyes, not yet.
I'm not trying to frighten you.
All I ask is that you think of me
not as a wish or a nightmare, but as a story
you have to tell yourselves –
not with an ending
in which everyone lives happily ever after,
or a B-movie apocalypse,
but maybe starting with the line
'To be continued...'
and see what happens next.
Remember this; I am not
written in stone
but in time –

so please don't shrug and say
what can we do,
it's too late, etc, etc, etc...
Already I hear the sound of seats
flipping and clapping as you head for the exit signs.
I feel like the comedian who died.

Dear mortals,
you are such strange creatures
with your greed and your kindness,
and your hearts like broken toys;
you carry fear with you everywhere
like a tiny god
in its box of shadows.
You love shopping and music
and good food.
You lie to yourselves
because you're afraid of the dark.
But the truth is this: you are in my hands
and I am in yours.
We are in this together,
face to face and eye to eye,
we are made for each other.
Now those of you who are still here;
open your eyes and tell me what you see.

Grace

(for Tansy Davies)

There was grace from the start

JOHN BERGER

Perhaps she follows the light
across the threshold admitting her
into darkness. She's alone,
or at the head of an elite delegation
processing with ceremony,
or with an audience of all ages
congregating, scared, thrilled
by the supremacy of dark;
She steps forward, listening
for the steps of an echo path
guiding her to the chamber; flame
in a jack-straws of sticks construes
shadows vaulting; now her fluent fingers
make deer flee and salmon leap,
and stick figures stampede
in a hullaballoo of hooves and cries.
She holds a fine stone blade
between two fingers, taps –
and a ghost bird flutters
free above their heads, then soars
into the secret of the rock.
Dark's her medium; she whispers
into the bowl of the wall,
hums, and the rock invokes
spirits answering, singing behind her back.
Perhaps now she lays her hand on the locked
door of stone and from her lips

blows ochre powder –
her hand, delicate as a leaf,
and another, and then another
fixed; and when she steps back
the hands remain, waving, signing
Grace was here, forever. Then,
she gathers the shadows and walks
back up the path into the point
of light.

Send

Ten hours ahead, my summer day's your night.
You and your phone are sleeping at home in London
under the Marimekko flowers of the winter duvet
while I'm walking the Coogee cliff path in the sun.

But we can share this via the satellites,
our mystery necromancers, constant stars
congregating signals and alerts,
reports of hurricanes and updates of wars

as the world turns underneath, dark into light,
relaying the miracle of our transmissions
from every megalopolis and beauty spot,
our jokes, news, clichés, love, emoticons –

the babble of our voices in the cloud.
I know they say we love what we must lose,
but this poem will not have that ending;
impossible intimacies, distances, but see

what I see; waves carry swimmers in their shimmer,
dogs walk owners, the nesting beach-crowd
like a colony of strangers in a dream...
I tap *I miss you XX* – then press *send*

Life on Earth

(The Voyager 1 spacecraft, launched 1977)

> This is a present from a small, distant world, a token of our
> sounds, our science, our images, our music, our thoughts,
> and our feelings. We are attempting to survive our time so
> we may live into yours...
>
> JIMMY CARTER

At the last moment
you turned to look back over your shoulder
for a final snapshot to send home; each single pixel
wired at the speed of light

took five hours to reach Earth –
and so we saw ourselves for the first time
no more than a scintilla in the blurry star-field
of our local heaven.

But those who created you
are fading with the age of analogue,
and the future is quickly bleaching the blue ball
bone-white...

So turn away, keep going
my tin-foil star, my ark, my Voyager,
beyond where the light thins into the boundless dark
with the immortal gold LP

fixed on your side,
coded for ancient technology, our message
of the sounds of life on earth, all that we are
or wish to seem –

thunder, surf, frogs,
cars, birds, footsteps, fire, Morse Code,
greetings in 55 languages, a kiss, a heartbeat,
laughter...

44,000 nightfall years
to the next star – so when our data stream
has long gone silent, and our cities turned to dust,
listen to what's out there –

the foundries of the stars,
a neutron's chant, whistling plasma waves,
a black hole's perturbations, dark matter's hush, the radiant
cantus firmus of the Big Bang,

and the whispers of the dead
from the far side of spacetime without end.
And when your heart's half-life decays to final silence
you'll carry the code of music –

Bach, Stravinsky, Chuck Berry,
initiation and wedding songs, Mariachi bands,
the Navajo night chant of healing and balance
against the harrowing winter,

and Blind Willie Johnson,
'Dark was the Night and Cold was the Ground,'
through the white noise of lost time and the event horizon
of that old black disc –

bottleneck slide guitar
played with a knife, blues, wordless, keened, howled
to the stars' responding congregation –
Ah oh, ah oh... mmmm... Lord...

Fragile

I'm singing in the rain!

He croons, eyes closed, crossed-legged
on a cardboard box broken down
to the outline of a bed, a raft in the dark

I'm sitting in the rain!

on a sea of shining pavement; a smaller
box with the recycle triangle icon holds
a can for coins, and later perhaps his head

I'm sleeping in the rain!

but the edges are dissolving in the tide, and only
FRAGILE taped crisscross over and over
is holding it all provisionally together.

Stranger Thing

(The Whitechapel fatberg, c/o the Museum of London)

Chip fat, cold shits, dead paints, hate mail, grease,
used wet-wipes, condoms, nappies, cotton buds,
paracetamol, toenail-crescents, needles, hair –

the dregs, swill, scum, muck, slop we flush away
are harvest festival for the moony monster
who rules the empire of the upside down

beneath the illusion of floorboards, parks and streets;
stranger thing, behemoth, lonely ogre, shy
Caliban created by our multitudes,

dreaming where the sewers slowly flow
through whispering galleries and gargoyle crypts,
bringing offerings to the awful sanctuary.

We sent our heroes down in hazmat suits
to besiege it; now these abominable lumps
festering in sealed and chilled vitrines

on live-feed for the curiosity of the world
are all that's left. The glass holds our reflections,
the beautiful ones who love to scare ourselves,

taking selfies with the alien bogey-beast,
our nightmare mirror image even now
regenerating in the dark beneath our feet.

Colibri

(humming bird)

Through a stitch in time, from a corner of thin air,
if you're not watching, he might appear

like the thousand pages of a tiny codex
flickered though a hundred times a heartbeat, shimmer-

frequencies of viridian, gold and turquoise,
his staring eye a needlepoint of ink –

yet if you look directly, nothing's there
but the drops of last night's rain glimmering

in the dark leaves of the flowering lemon tree.

The Back of Your Head

Stranger, I'm looking at the back of your head;
at the heart of the crown
where the whorl starts;
at the touch of skin
like the stars
clustered at the core of a spiral galaxy,
curls whirling out in points of light on dark
to infinity and beyond…

There are more than 170 billion galaxies
in the observable universe –
but on the top deck of this bus the greatest mystery
is the dark matter of your eyes
which I shall never see –
as you will never read this little poem.

NOTES

Maenad (13)
In Greek mythology, maenads were the female followers of Dionysus. Their name literally translates as 'raving ones'.

Still life: Plastic Water Bottle (used) (15)
Around 35.8 million plastic bottles are used every day in the UK, but only 19.8 million are recycled. This means there are on average 16 million plastic bottles a day not making their way into the recycling bin. Instead, they are put into landfill, burnt or leak into the environment and oceans. Plastics are now found everywhere from the Arctic to Antarctica. They pollute every natural system, and microplastics are found in an increasing number of organisms, including humans.

Driving to Achiltibue (36)
The Gaelic refrain is from Capercaillie's 'Puirt A Buel'

The Dancing Satyr (45)
The over-life-size *Dancing Satyr* is a Greek bronze statue. The torso was recovered from the sandy sea floor at a depth of 500 m off the southwestern coast of Sicily on the night of 4 March 1998, in the nets of a fishing boat. It is dated to approximately 3rd or 2nd centuries BCE.

Arctic Poems II (49)
Ice core samples are drilled from ice sheets, the Antarctic ice cap and glaciers to provide a climactic record of atmospheric composition going back hundreds of thousands of years.

Grace (55)
Ancient hand stencils and handprints have been found in caves in Argentina, Africa, Borneo, Australia, and in the 12,000- to

40,000-year-old cave paintings of southern France and northern Spain. A recent analysis proposes many of the hand prints may be female, suggesting that cave artists were mostly women.

Life on Earth (56)
The Voyager programme is a NASA scientific project to study the outer Solar System. Both Voyager 1 and 11 were launched in 1977. On 25 August 2012, Voyager 1 became the first human-made object to cross the heliosphere, a bubble-like region of space dominated by the sun, and to enter interstellar space, traveling 'further than anyone, or anything, in history'. Each craft carries a Golden Record, a phonograph containing sounds and images selected to portray the diversity of life, knowledge and culture on Earth, and are intended for any intelligent extra-terrestrial life form who may find them.

Stranger Thing (59)
A fatberg is a huge, congealed lump of oil, rubbish and waste which blocks the sewers beneath a city. The largest fatberg recorded was under Whitechapel. It is estimated to have weighed 130 tonnes – two jumbo jets – and was 250 metres long. The Museum of London conserved and displayed samples of it in *Fatberg!* (2018). Vyki Sparkes, the curator, noted: *It's grand, magnificent, fascinating and disgusting. The perfect museum object!*